Beauty Shop Talk

Talk

Musings from behind the Chair

Rhonda Trosky

WestBow Press books may be ordered through booksellers or by contacting:

WestBow Press
A Division of Thomas Nelson & Zondervan
1663 Liberty Drive
Bloomington, IN 47403
www.westbowpress.com
844-714-3454

MSG:
Scripture taken from The Message. Copyright © 1993, 1994, 1995, 1996, 2000, 2001, 2002. Used by permission of NavPress Publishing Group.

NIV:
Scripture quotations taken from The Holy Bible, New International Version® NIV® Copyright © 1973 1978 1984 2011 by Biblica, Inc. TM. Used by permission. All rights reserved worldwide.

ISBN: 978-1-6642-3292-1 (sc)
ISBN: 978-1-6642-3294-5 (hc)
ISBN: 978-1-6642-3293-8 (e)

Library of Congress Control Number: 2021908762

Print information available on the last page.

WestBow Press rev. date: 09/08/2021

WESTBOW
P R E S S®
A DIVISION OF THOMAS NELSON
& ZONDERVAN

This is for you, Mom. Thanks for sharing the art of making others feel beautiful. Working with you, Mom, always meant joy, laughter, cutting, curling, coloring, styling, and counseling our clients—precious moments as a mother and daughter team. Thank you, Pam Lee, for helping me to create my radio segment into a coffee-table book. Your patience, kindness, and lifelong friendship is a gift.

Highlights

Getting your hair colored or highlighted is different for each person. Certain clients do not want their hair to look like it has been colored. They prefer the more natural look. They want me to create really soft, natural-looking highlights. I'm like, "Who wants to look natural?" Of course I am in the business of creativity.

This brings me to scripture. Physical appearance is important to God in that it reveals the glory of his creative abilities. God crafted each of us to look exactly as we do for his own perfect reasons.

> Before I formed you in the womb I knew you, before you were born I set you apart. (Jeremiah 1:5)

God places some value on appearance. If he did not, we would all look the same. God gave us creative minds, so I say, "Enjoy, have fun, and be creative with your hair."

Fresh Start

Why do people bring in an old photo of their hair from twenty years ago and say, "I really like my hair in the picture. Can you cut my hair like this?" I look at the photo and I'm like, "OK, sure. I can do that, but you have no wrinkles in this picture. If you think your face is going to look twenty years younger, you might be surprised by the results."

Second Corinthians 5:17 says, "Therefore, if anyone is in Christ, he is a new creation, the old has gone and the new has come!"

Friends, you are a brand-new person. Let's leave that old hairdo in the picture, and go for a fresh new do!

Gray Hair

Many clients come to the shop asking, "What can I do with these gray hairs coming in?" "I am young and getting so many gray hairs," or, "I know I'm not young, but I'm not ready to be gray." What do I tell my clients who want to color their gray roots? "Absolutely. I can cover that up with hair color. As a matter of fact, you will look ten years younger."

Proverbs 16:31 says, "Gray hair is a crown of splendor: it is attained by a righteous life."

Friends, gray hairs are not a sign of disgrace to be covered over; they are a crown of splendor. As you look in the mirror and find more and more "splendor," count them as God's reward for a loyal life faithful to him. Praise him, and thank him that you even have hair.

Perfect Hair Products

I am often asked, "What professional products do you prefer?" Most often, the answer depends on what type of hair the person has. Is your hair thick, or is it fine? Do you have curly or straight hair? Oily or dry? Different products work differently with your individual hair type. With so many products on the market, it becomes quite confusing as to which product will work best on your hair.

The Lord our God is not one of confusion.

> One Lord, one faith, one baptism; one God and Father of all, who is over all and through all and in all. (Ephesians 4:5–6)

We are all so lucky we have one product to choose from. That is God, our Father, who is in every believer's life. It is an easy choice; you don't have to shop the market. He is ready and waiting to be the product you reach for every day.

Praying for the Stylist

Have you ever thought about praying before you get a haircut? "Oh, Lord, please don't let her go crazy on me and cut all my hair off. Don't let her talk me into something I know I will not like." Or, "Lord, please put your handiwork in her hands so I come out looking OK." You know, you might want to start praying before entering a salon.

Hear the sound of my cry, my King, and my God, for to you do I pray. (Psalm 5:2)

God is far too creative to teach every person on earth to interact with him through prayer in exactly the same way. He is the one who designed us all differently and delights in our distinctiveness. Ask God to teach you to pray and to talk and listen to God in ways that are best for you. You are God's unique creation. Celebrate that in your life and in your prayers.

Aging

Our appearance can change significantly as we get older, and not always in the ways we would expect. Many people associate aging with the appearance of fine lines and wrinkles on the face, but your hair can show your age too. Though gray hairs are an expected part of aging, you may be surprised to find that your hair gets coarser and can get kinky as you get older.

Is not wisdom found among the aged: Does not long life bring wisdom? (Job 12:12)

If you are discouraged by your kinky, gray, coarse hair, take this advice from Job: "Wisdom is found among the aged."

Using Your Talent

From the time many stylists are children, they dream of doing hair. They generally have a passion for making others look their best, using their creativity to accomplish this. Schooling for cosmetology is great. You are trained to use your style and talent to correct and change, helping clients to see the best in what they have.

> From infancy you have known the holy scriptures which are able to make you wise, for salvation through faith in Christ Jesus. All scripture is God-breathed and is useful for teaching, rebuking, correcting and training in righteousness so that the man of God may be thoroughly equipped for every good work. (2 Timothy 3:15)

Just as schooling equips us for our careers, the Word of God equips us and guides us in our God-given talents, preparing us to help others see the best in what they have.

Shampoo Bowl

You know that feeling when your hair is being shampooed at the salon? It feels so good! You wonder why you don't feel that same magic when you shampoo your own hair. I have clients who say this—the head massage—is the best part of getting their hair cut. Some will say, "I will pay you more if you will shampoo a little longer."

> Soak me in your laundry and I will come out clean. Scrub me and I'll have a snow-white life. (Psalm 51:7 MSG)

When we scrub our hair, we need to ask God to cleanse us from within, clearing our hearts and spirits for new thoughts and desires. Right conduct can come only from a clean heart and spirit. Ask God to cleanse a pure heart and spirit in you today.

My, What Big Ears You Have

Many of my clients are very concerned about their ears showing. They either feel like they are too big or that they stick out like Dumbo's ears. Either way, some clients do not want their ears to show. So I must not cut their hair over the ears. It is true as we age the collagen and elastin fibers that create cartilage begin to break down. This causes our ears to stretch and sag, making them appear longer.

> The heart of the discerning acquires knowledge; the ears of the wise seek it out.
> (Proverbs 18:15)

Use your big ears to hear wisdom.

My Nana

You think that when you are ninety years old you might not really care about your hair, right? Not my nana. Her hair has always been important to her. It is so cool to have a grandmother who is still concerned about the way she presents herself. Maybe that is why I am in the beauty business. You know, the apple does not fall far from the tree.

And His mercy is on those who fear Him from generation to generation. (Luke 1:50)

How much do we really fear the Lord? It is not too late to produce better fruit. Whatever your age, wherever you are in life, there is always room for improvement. From generation to generation, the apple does not fall far from the tree.

Wigging Out

Do you ever look at your hair and say, "Maybe I should just get a wig"? Have you ever felt that way? I have many times. I have even tried on wigs and thought, *How nice it would be to just put this on and go.* Then you start thinking about all the what-ifs. What if the wind blows it off? What if it gets stuck on something and comes off? What if someone notices that I am wearing a wig?

> Have I not commanded you? Be strong and courageous. Do not be terrified, or do not be discouraged, for the Lord your God will be with you wherever you go. (Joshua 1:9)

Our God is always with us, so I say quit with the what-ifs. Put the wig on and go!

Sunday Church

Times have not changed much from when I was a child. I remember my mother curling mine and my sister's hair on pink sponge rollers. We would sleep in them every Saturday night so our hair would look nice for Sunday church. To this day, clients still frequent the shop on Saturdays, so their hair looks nice for Sunday church.

> So here's what I want you to do, God helping you. Take your everyday ordinary life—your sleeping, eating, going-to-work, and walking around life—and place it before God as an offering. Embracing what God does for you is the best thing you can do for him. (Romans 12:1 MSG)

Do this out of gratitude that our sins have been forgiven. Bless you, my friends, as you prepare your time with the Lord for Sunday church.

Beauty Rituals

Are you like me, feeling overwhelmed at the beauty rituals we put ourselves through? Like before you go to bed, you need to remove all your makeup; put the zit cream on and then the antiwrinkle cream; brush and floss your teeth so you don't get gingivitis; and don't forget your retainer! Then we wake up, and we need to condition our hair, moisturize our skin, use the bleach toothpaste to whiten our teeth, and then apply sunscreen so we don't get cancer.

> Come to me all you who are weary and burdened and I will give you rest. (Matthew 11:28)

Isn't it nice to know you can go to Jesus when you are tired and burned out? Jesus reminds us, "Get away with me and I will show you, real rest. Keep company with me and you'll learn to live freely and lightly." Ooooh, I believe that is just what I need—to learn to live "freely and lightly."

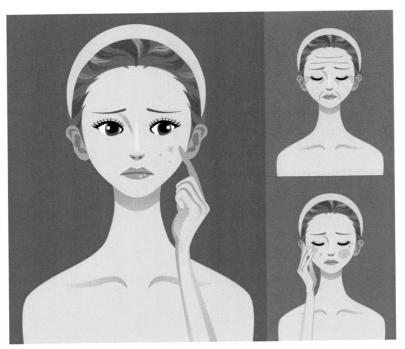

To Cut or Not to Cut, That Is the Question

When it comes to many women, hair is a big deal. Should you cut it? Should you just trim it? Should you color your hair? If you do, should you go dark or light? The list goes on and on. And I, being in the hair industry, suffer the same pain. What to do with the hair?

Scripture advises to wait for peace when in doubt about our decisions.

> I will listen to what God the Lord will say, for He will speak peace to his people.
> (Psalm 85:8)

Whenever you make a decision and believe you hear God speak, use the scale of peace. If you do not have peace with the guidance you have heard, don't proceed with it. Always wait to do what you think God has instructed you to do until peace fills your soul. Peace gives us confidence and faith. Wait for peace before you act.

A Work of Art

When you are sitting in the chair at the salon, most of the time you are watching diligently how the stylist is fixing your hair. You often then buy the shampoo and conditioner she used. You might even purchase the exact brush and curling iron she used and then the voluminous hair gel and hairspray. The next day your effort to duplicate her artwork on your head comes to a quick disappointment.

Isn't it nice to know that we don't have to work so hard to be in Christ? It doesn't cost us a thing.

> It is for freedom that Christ has set us free. Stand firm, then, and do not let yourselves be burdened again by a yoke of slavery. (Galatians 5:1)

Christ died to set us free from sin and from a long list of laws and regulations. We do not have to purchase products to be in God's favor. God's gift is free, eternal life delivered by Jesus, our Master.

Balding

How about that hair falling out? You know, when you shower and there is hair all around the drain, and you are like, "Seriously, is that my hair?" Then you comb it, and sure enough, more hair comes out. You start to think, *If this keeps up, I will be bald!* You research the internet about why you are losing hair, and basically it says, "Stress." So what are you supposed to do? Divorce your spouse, quit your job, and give away the kids?

We all suffer from stress but God says,

> Let not your heart be troubled, believe in God, believe also in me. (John 14:1)

So friends, how can we get away from stress? We can learn that worrying will not change the situation. But believing God knows all our problems, we can quiet our minds of our troubles. He reminds us of the importance of trusting him.

Unwanted Hair

Why is it that the older we get the more hair grows in places we don't need hair growing, like our noses or our ears? For some of us, our eyebrows get longer. It is just so unattractive. Even the hair on our toes grows. First it starts out on our big toe, and then gradually you start seeing hair on your second toe. And before long, we are shaving off hair from all our toes. It is so annoying.

> So God created man in his own image, in the image of God he created him; male and female he created them. (Genesis 1:27)

God knew what he was doing when he created us in his image. So even when we see hair growing in places we do not necessarily find attractive, we know that the Creator of this world has a design far above what our minds can conceive. So probably the best thing is to thank him for his wonderful design and for creating us in his image.

Mind, Body, and Soul

Today is the first day of the new year! Wow, time to start the diet and exercise program. Six weeks to a new body! Get your body in shape by Valentine's Day. Then there is the advertisement, "How to grow your hair three inches in a month." Seriously, we all know those are gimmicks, but we still purchase the products hoping for the results they claim.

> Proverbs 14:30 says, "A sound mind makes for a robust body but runaway emotions corrode the bones."

Friends, do not let the headlines of the magazines at the checkout stands go against what you know is the truth. If you want to lose weight and grow your hair out, then you must get control over your mind. That is where all change starts.

Perfect Hair

Why do clients come to the shop complaining that they just cannot fix their hair the way the stylist does? Well of course not. You cannot stand behind yourself and fix your hair the way we do. It is difficult. If you could take your head off and put it on a stand to fix it like you can a wig, it would be a bit easier. So yes, I understand you're feeling inadequate about styling your hair as well as your stylist does.

> "Consider it pure joy, my brothers, whenever you face trials of many kinds because you know that the testing of your faith develops perseverance." Perseverance must finish its work so that you maybe mature and complete, not lacking in anything. (James 1:2)

As you struggle to perfect your hair, just know that you are maturing and being made complete, lacking in nothing.

Hat Day

I love hats, especially when it is a bad hair day. You know those days when your hair is just not turning out the way you hoped, or when you are in a hurry and do not have time to fix your hair. There is nothing better than being able to throw on a hat and go.

The one who rocks the hat is Jesus Christ. He is our protector and our covering through good and bad days.

> The Lord is my rock, my fortress, and my deliverer, my God is my rock, in whom I take refuge, my shield and the horn of my salvation. (2 Samuel 22:3)

Whether it is a good or a bad hair day, one thing is for certain: we all can rock the hat of Jesus Christ.

Damaged Hair

Why do so many people spend so much money on their hair? Well for one thing, they are told they need to. To which I say yes, taking care of your hair is important. You need to trim your ends to keep your hair looking healthy and promote new growth. It is important to condition the hair and treat it with products to help keep its glow. And, of course, it is always nice to have good-smelling hair.

> I am the true vine and my Father is the gardener. He cuts off every branch in me that bears no fruit. (John 15:5)

God, at times, must discipline us to strengthen our character and faith. Branches that do not bear fruit are cut off. They are worthless, often infecting the rest of the tree. Just as damaged hair affects the rest of our hair, we need to cut it off. Allow God to trim you spiritually to promote new growth.

Bangs

Why is it that cutting our bangs is such a big deal? When your bangs are all one length, it is so hard to decide to cut them. And when we do, we are so excited. Then we go home, and no one says a thing. You are like, "Hey, do you notice something different about me?" Your friends or family look at you and ask, "Did you get glasses?" You answer, "No! I got bangs!"

> Praise be to the name of God for ever and ever, wisdom and power are his, He changes times and seasons. (Daniel 2:21)

As God is in the business of change, I believe cutting our bangs for a new look is great advice from your stylist, but if you want real change in your life, start by asking God for wisdom. God gives wisdom freely to all who ask. That is where real change begins.

Purple Hair

It is so fun to put vibrant color in our hair. Today my client wanted purple. She had dark hair. When your hair is dark, you must bleach it to replace it with a vibrant color. After several steps and much time processing, my client walked away with rich, deep purple highlights in her hair. It was beautiful!

> This reminds me of the virtuous woman: "She makes coverings for her bed; she is clothed in fine linen and purple" (Proverbs 31:22).

It is obvious that purple is a great color. A smart, worthy, noble woman may choose to adorn her hair with purple highlights. Vibrant hair color is fun and makes for a good time anticipating the results. So I said to my client, "Good choice. I think purple might be one of God's favorite colors."

Split Ends

I had a client come to the beauty shop and ask, "What can I do with these split ends? I love my long hair. I have tried everything from professional beauty products to over-the-counter product to coconut oil." I am looking at her, thinking, *Hmmm. You would look much younger with short hair.*

This scripture came to mind.

> Cut your hair off and throw it away. (Jeremiah 7:29)

Just like our hair, our lives are always splitting at the ends. We need to cut off and throw away all that is not bringing glory to our Father. Take time to trim your spiritual ends so you can continue growing and maturing in God's love.

Mirror, Mirror

So here we are, a few days before the big event. Have you looked in the mirror? When you finally have time to look at yourself, you may be filled with horror and wonder, *When was the last time I went to the salon? How did the time get away? Will I be able to get an appointment to tame this wild hair before the party?*

> Your beauty should not come from outward adornment, such as braided hair and wearing of gold jewelry and fine clothes. Instead, It should be that of your inner self, the unfading beauty of a gentle and quiet spirit, which is of great worth in God's sight. (1 Peter 3:3, 4)

I do love this scripture, but for the sake of your friends and relatives who have to look at you, please present yourself appropriately.

Live Free

Have you ever noticed the commercials with the convertibles and the people in the car? Their hair is blowing in the wind perfectly; the sun is shining on their faces. Aww, it just makes you want to drive a convertible. But no! When I drive one, the wind blows my hair completely in my face, out of control, and it sticks to my lip gloss. I end up looking like a tangled mess. Somehow I just do not get that superstar look.

> Keep your lives free from the love of money and be content with what you have because God has said, "Never will I leave you; never will I forsake you." (Hebrews 13:5)

So do not run out and buy a convertible thinking you are going to drive around looking like a superstar, because you probably won't. Be content with your windows rolled up and your hair in place. When you reach your final destination, God will be there waiting.

Daily Routine

I love the holidays and all that goes with them. But it is always nice to get back to some sort of a schedule. It seems when you are traveling and staying up late at night, the simple act of washing your face and brushing your teeth before going to bed gets pushed aside.

> Then he said to them all: "If anyone would come after me, he must deny himself and take up his cross daily and follow me." (Luke 9:23)

I like to emphasize the word "daily." Just like brushing our teeth and washing our faces, think about scheduling God into your daily beauty routine. When you spend time with the Lord on a daily basis, you reap the benefits of a clean mouth and body.

Listening Ear

In the salon, we often talk about having a bad boss or a leader with a lack of listening skills. Not listening is one of the biggest mistakes I believe leaders make. Leaders come in all facets— schoolteachers, business owners, pastors, managers, doctors, even your stylist. If you are not listening to your clients, you are probably not going to get the results you are looking for.

> Everyone should be quick to listen, slow to speak, and slow to become angry. (James 1:19)

If you want to be an effective leader, you need to be a good listener first. Keep track of how much you talk and how much you listen. When people talk with you, do they feel that their viewpoints and ideas have value? Probably the greatest reason people fail in leadership is not immorality or lack of intelligence but the fact that they are not good listeners.

Traditions

It is New Year's Eve. A tradition for some of my clients is to get their hair all done up for an evening of the fun and festivities while bringing in the new year. Do you have certain traditions on New Year's Eve? I remember as a child, when midnight struck, we would get our pots and pans, take them outside, and make all kinds of noise. It is nice to have traditions and to continue them with family and friends.

> So then brothers, stand firm and hold to the traditions we passed on to you.
> (2 Thessalonians 2:15)

As we begin the new year, stand firm, and hold on to the truth you have been taught. You will face pressure from worldliness to leave the faith. Stay true to Christ's teaching, passing it on to your children and grandchildren because our lives depend on it.

Wax Job

It seems more and more teen boys and girls are coming to the shop to get their eyebrows and any other unwanted facial hair waxed. It is actually fun to put hot wax between their eyes and clean the area of unwanted hair.

> As far as the east is from the west, he has removed our transgressions from us. (Psalm 103:12)

Friends, this is a portrait of God's forgiveness. God has wiped our record clean. Just as the hot wax removes unwanted hair, God has removed our sins and remembers them no longer. Take time to thank God for the removal of our sins pain-free—no hot wax required.

Redheads

Redheads run in my family. My dad had red hair; he was what they called a "carrottop." Generally speaking, redheads have fair skin and freckles. My mother hoped at least one of her children would carry on that genetic predisposition. Out of three children and five grandchildren, not one of us got that gene. Maybe through this next generation that recessive gene will pop up. I hope it does. I think redheads are special.

> For you are a people holy to the Lord your God. The Lord your God has chosen you out of all the peoples on the face of the earth to be his people, his treasured possession. (Deuteronomy 7:6)

For those of you with red hair, fair skin, and freckles, I think you are a treasured possession. Many clients pay high dollars to color their hair the way God colored yours.

A New Rx

How often do we go to the salon to get a different look? It is so exciting to anticipate the new look, whether it is getting bangs or layering our hair. Sometimes it is just as simple as trimming the dead ends off or curling your hair a little differently. It just makes you smile to leave the salon with a new hairdo.

A cheerful heart is good medicine. (Proverbs 17:22)

To be cheerful is to greet others with a warm welcome, a word of encouragement, and enthusiasm. Cheerfulness is having a positive outlook on the future. Such people are as welcome as pain-relieving medicine. So I say get your hair done. It cheers the soul and refreshes the spirit. I think it is good medicine.

Christmas Eve

It is Christmas Eve. There is just something about this evening that brings out the festive attire. It is time to put on that shiny dress, a bit of red lipstick, perhaps rhinestones in your hair, and the bow tie for your little guys. As we prepare for the evening with all the glitz, anticipation, and excitement, do not forget the camera. We have memories in the making.

> Charm can mislead and beauty soon fades, but a woman who fears the Lord is to be praised. (Proverbs 31:30)

As we gather with family for an evening of remembering the birth of our Savior, remember your attractiveness comes from your character, integrity, and compassion. As you pose for the camera, make sure your inner beauty is what lights up the picture.

Pedicure

In my salon we do hair only—no toenails, no fingernails, and no tanning bed. We just fix your hair. So when someone wants a pedicure, we refer them to a specialty shop for that treatment.

> Now that I, your Lord and Teacher, have washed your feet, you also should wash one another's feet. I have set you an example that you should do as I have done for you. (John 13:14)

The great thing about these specialty shops is that they concentrate on the feet and hands. We all have special gifts. Use them to bring glory to the Father.

Tangles

I am your hair; always have been, always will be. Some days you like me because I am so good. Some days you can't stand me because I am not doing what you want. Just remember God made these hairs on your head. He even knows how many of us there are. Don't let me—your hair—shake up what is going on around you. Instead of desperately trying to maintain and control me, relax and "shake it off."

> Let us throw off everything that hinders and the sins that so easily entangles. (Hebrews 12:1)

Learn to enjoy me more. Relax; wear a happy face. Walk through today with a childlike spirit, taking in every blessing God gives you. Focus on God, and enjoy life even with the messy hair because the whole world is watching you.

Firming Gel

There are so many products to choose from when it comes to styling your hair that it can get confusing. When your hair is short and you want it to stand up and stay put, you have to use a strong product. Root lifter lifts your roots. Then there is mousse, paste, gel, cream, sprays, and wax.

> Come near to God and he will come near to you. (James 4:8)

Just like our hair, if you want your relationship with God to stand strong, if you want him to work in you and be with you at all times, you must come near to Him. How can you come near to God? James says to submit to God, yield to his authority, and commit your life to him and his control. There is no better product than Jesus Christ.

HAIR CARE SET

Botox

Clients often come in and show me a picture of the winner of *America's Top Model* and ask, "Can you make me look like this?" Well, for starters, this girl may have had a lot of Botox, spent many hours in the tanning bed, and been worked over by several design stylists and makeup artists. After her photo shoot, her pictures have been edited for perfection.

> I will give thanks to you for I am fearfully and wonderfully made; wonderful are your works. (Psalm 139:14)

Friends, in our moments of insecurity, remember we are wonderfully made by God.

Resting

Summer break for students means they are free from schoolwork. It is a great time to get the kids in for haircuts. We want our children to enjoy the break and have fun with their time off, but many parents struggle with time off or what we often refer to as "wasted time," feeling that if we are not accomplishing something, then we are being lazy.

> The Lord is my shepherd, I will not be in want. He makes me lie down in green pastures, he leads me beside quiet waters, he restores my soul. (Psalms 23: 1-2)

Scripture is telling you to take some time out to enjoy what God has given you. Spend some free time with your children. The time you enjoy wasting is not wasted time.

Sweeping

Cleaning a beauty shop full of hair is not always an easy task. At the end of the day, after standing on my feet and pleasing people all day, the last thing I want to do is clean up the mess I have made. We often leave work at the end of a busy day wiped out.

> Let us not become weary in doing good, for at the proper time we will reap a harvest if we do not give up. (Galatians 6:9)

Just be the best you, thanking God always and trusting him for the results.

Set the Timer

Springtime makes you want to hit the tanning beds to get a little color before summer. If you have never used a tanning bed, the first time you do is kind of weird. You stand there thinking, *Do I tan in a swimsuit, or do I tan naked? Do I use tanning lotion, or do I just dive into that hot bed?* Then, once you are in there, it is weird just lying there. I find, for me, it is a good time to pray.

Pray continually. (1 Thessalonians 5:17)

You have set the timer for anywhere from ten to twenty minutes. It is actually a good time to just talk to the Lord. It is a peaceful, quiet time until, of course, the buzzer goes off and startles you into realizing you are done baking.

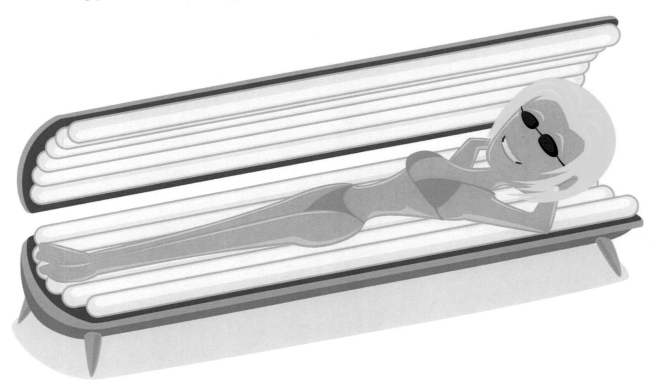

Money

As a hairdresser, you come home many times with hair on your clothes, down your shirt, in your boots—everywhere. At times my kids have said, "Mom, that is so gross." My reply is, "The more hair on me, the more money I made." Which means tonight we might eat dinner out. Now that is an idea everybody likes.

> Then Jesus declared, "I am the bread of life. He who comes to me will never go hungry, and he who believes in me will never be thirsty." (John 6:35)

How much time do you spend sustaining your spiritual life? Do others see the "bread of life" in you? Invite Christ into your daily walk to sustain spiritual life, and you will never go hungry.

Leaders

One of the topics discussed in the shop is leadership. A leader can be defined as someone people follow or someone who guides or directs others. If you are a leader in your line of work, or if you are a parent, this one small act can help you in your leadership. It is called affirmation and praise.

Therefore, encourage one another and build each other up. (1 Thessalonians 5:11)

Everyone thrives on affirmation and praise. Since we were children, we have all loved to get praise for a job well done. Our need for affirmation does not diminish as we grow older! For many people, encouraging words give them the fuel to go on even in the most intense work environments. Show love to your workers, and they will follow you anywhere.

Static Hair

Do you ever get ready to go out and your makeup looks great, your clothes are perfect, nails are beautiful, but you are just not happy with your hair? You keep returning to the mirror. Your hair is not lying right, or it has a messy look. By now you have worked with it for so long that is has static electricity. It is driving you crazy. It becomes your whole focus.

Let us fix our eyes on Jesus, the author, and perfecter of our faith. (Hebrews 12:2)

The Lord says the only way to fix your balance is to fix your eyes on him. If you gaze too long at your hair, you will become dizzy and confused. Refresh yourself in his presence, and your eyes will be steady and sure.

Shades of Gray

One of the colors that is trending right now is gray. You might not believe that young girls want to color their hair gray, but they do. If done right, it looks great. There are several different shades depending on your skin color and natural hair color that work well.

> Youth may be admired for strength, but gray hair gives prestige to old age. (Proverbs 20:29)

So I am guessing our youth want to be strong and wise when choosing to go gray. Who would have ever thought there could be a different meaning to *50 Shades of Grey*?

Wind Blown

Have you ever come in from a strong wind, looked at your hair, and thought, *Wow, it looks kind of cute*? So you try to fix it like that. Sometimes it's something as small as brushing your bangs in a different direction or the sides of your hair either away from your face or toward your face. It is just a small detail, but you liked the look the wind gave your hair, and you try to reproduce it.

> Praise the Lord from the earth, you great sea creatures and all ocean depths, lightning and hail, snow and clouds, stormy winds fulfilling his word. (Psalm 148:7–8)

So much of the time wind is not our friend, but we can remember to thank God for the wind in times of new hairdos. If not for the wind, we might not see the new look God can create with his power. And through his power, he changes us.

New Year's Resolution

Are you ready? Ready for the new year? Are you making a New Year's resolution? I hate New Year's resolutions. I never stick with them. I do not seem to ever follow through. Chatting with many of my clients, they have the same problem. So why make a resolution?

I can do all things through Christ who gives me strength. (Philippians 4:13)

Can we really do everything? In our daily lives, we will face troubles, pressures, and trials. As they come, ask Christ to strengthen you. The Lord our God is the Master of perfection, and through his strength, we are able to do all things in regard to his interest. So bring in the new year with a Christ-centered resolution.

Grace Undeserved

In the beauty business, as in any business, there can be a lot of jealousy, backstabbing, and stealing of clients. Hairdressers may feel their work is superior and would rather not associate with someone they consider a less-skilled stylist. Just because one stylist does it one way does not necessarily mean that it is the only way to do hair.

> For it is by grace you have been saved, through faith and this not from yourselves, it is the gift of God not by works, so that no one can boast. For we are God's workmanship, created in Christ Jesus to do good works, which God prepared in advance for us to do. (Ephesians 2: 8-10)

In all situations, including those that are job-related, we often come to a time when we must choose between good and evil and do what is just and right. This is the core of Christian living. If we have experienced God's grace, we will want to pass it on to others. And remember, grace is undeserved favor.

Messy Maverick

One of the biggest mistakes made by leaders is their inability to understand a "maverick." A maverick is an individual who does not go along with a group or party. Many stylists are mavericks. Large organizations tend to kill off mavericks before they can take root. We must learn how to recognize useful mavericks and make them part of our teams.

We have different gifts according to the grace given us. (Romans 12:6)

Over time, our man-made organizations grow old, rigid, and tired—just like we humans do. The pioneering spirit of mavericks can stop that slide and turn it around. Mavericks make messes by their very natures. But these are the good messes organizations need. You will be amazed what a new face can bring to a stagnant group of people.

Natural Curl

Those of you with naturally curly hair often say, "It would be nice if I had the same curl all over my head." Many people with all those curls do have certain areas of their hair where the curls are drastically different. It is almost straight in some areas. So it does take a lot of work to get the curls to look even all around your head.

> Do everything without complaining or arguing, so that you may become blameless and pure, children of God with out fault in a crooked and depraved generation, in which you shine like stars in the universe. (Philippians 2:14)

As you work on your hair, curling the straight part so all your curls look the same, be a breath of fresh air in this polluted society. Be living proof that you didn't do all that work for nothing. Provide people with a glimpse of good living and a loving God.

Perm

Why is it that right before we have a surgical procedure or we know we are not going to be able to spend much time on our hair we decide to get a perm? You know—the curly kind. You think you can just pick it out, so it will be easy to work with. It's a great feeling to leave the salon with the curl in our hair. But then suddenly, we get home and start questioning, "Why did I get a perm? I hate these curls."

Do not let any unwholesome talk come out of your mouths. (Ephesians 4:29)

So do not curse your new curls. Be content with the choice to perm your hair, and do not second-guess your decision.

Bed Head

Why is it when we wake up we have bed head—especially if we go to bed with our hair damp? If you have a cowlick, well, that is worse. Your hair is sticking up in places that only gel and a wire brush can contain. From the *Merriam-Webster Dictionary*, the definition of "cowlick" is a small bunch of hair on a person's head that sticks up above the hair around it and will not lie flat.

> This calls for patient endurance on the part of the saints who obey God's commandments and remain faithful to Jesus. (Revelation 14:12)

Just as scripture calls us to be patient and to remain faithful to God, be patient with your cowlicks. Learn to work with them, not against them. Patience is a virtue!

Printed in the United States
by Baker & Taylor Publisher Services